Little Legends

EXCEPTIONAL MEN

IN

BLACK HISTORY

Little Legends

EXCEPTIONAL MEN

IN

BLACK HISTORY

VASHTI HARRISON

with KWESI JOHNSON

Little, Brown and Company

New York Boston

ABOUT THIS BOOK

The illustrations for this book were done in Adobe Photoshop. This book was edited by Farrin Jacobs and designed by David Caplan and Kelly Brennan. The production was supervised by Erika Schwartz, and the production editor was Jen Graham. The text was set in Today SB, and the display type is True North.

TO THOSE WHO AIM TO BE

NOT JUST GREAT

BUT ALSO GOOD.

—VH

TO ONE OF THE BEST BROTHERS

A GUY COULD HAVE,

A TRUE LEGEND, PATEN LOCKE.

—KJ

Contents

Introduction

This book almost didn't exist. Many people asked for it, but for a long time I didn't think I was the right person to create it. I knew I didn't feel the same way about telling men's stories that I did about women's. But I knew other authors might, and I would root on the sidelines for their books.

In many ways, I made my first book, *Little Leaders: Bold Women in Black History,* for my younger self. I wanted to share the stories of incredible African American women who did amazing things across different fields of study because I needed it. The book became very personal, and I connected with the stories on a deep level. And, to be honest, in my research I found book after book and documentary after documentary that highlighted the stories of men over women, so I didn't feel a sense of urgency and necessity to write about them. But still I kept hearing the requests. And finally I was able to see how I could answer.

In the years since *Little Leaders* was published, I have worked on other projects and grown as an author and artist and come to understand that this book may not be for me or my younger self, but that doesn't make it any less necessary. When I began to see it from this perspective, I found the passion and excitement to research and write and draw. I wanted to provide others with the experience I had with *Little Leaders*.

My first book was inspired by Black History Month. When Carter G. Woodson founded Negro History Week in 1926, his main message was to celebrate the stories that had been neglected throughout history. For that reason, in this book I chose to tell the stories of exceptional men you don't see too often in the mainstream. A survey of important black men often lists the same people: Martin Luther King Jr., Nelson Mandela, Barack Obama, Jackie Robinson, Malcolm X, among others. I took this opportunity to give space to men like Robert Smalls and John Robinson, leaders and dreamers who don't have stacks of books written about them. Of course, I included some big-name figures as well, in case this might be someone's first introduction to black history. It was a delicate balancing act! Overall, though, I wanted to tell the stories of exceptional men. Yes, they were better than average and unusually good, but to me *exceptional* in this case also suggests exceptions to the expectations for black men in today's society.

The men in these pages were leaders, trailblazers, and pioneers in their fields, usually the first wherever they went. They defied stereotypes and expectations. Sure, they were bold and brave when necessary, but they were also kind and compassionate. People like Charles Henry Turner and Charles R. Drew were educators, dedicated to sharing their knowledge and discoveries with the next generation. Both Marshall "Major" Taylor and André Leon Talley broke ground in fields you wouldn't necessarily associate with black men: cycling and women's fashion. They made a place for themselves and for other people of color when it meant making themselves targets. All too often, these men had to overcome racism to get where they went, but when they got there, they did incredible things. They had to be resilient and tough at times, but they were defined by their passion, patience, and goodness. And for that they are legendary.

I see this book as a sibling to my first, but I don't think of this as "the boy book" or a book for boys. My books are for all readers. Here, I feature the stories of men, but they are *for* everyone, just as *Little Leaders* is. Whoever you are, there is a story for you in the pages that follow. The Little Legends are here to guide you on this journey throughout history. Let them inspire your future!

Benjamin Banneker
1731 – 1806

INVENTOR, FARMER

Although Benjamin attended school for only a few years before working on his father's farm, he loved to read and study. He became so good at math that people came from all around Maryland to test him with questions. They were amazed at how quickly he answered them. He would ask math questions, too, writing them as poems.

Benjamin wanted to use his abilities to help people. At fifteen, he created an irrigation system that kept water flowing to his farm's crops. It was so effective that even during droughts, the Banneker farm flourished. In 1753, he became fascinated with a friend's watch. Watches were rare at that time, and his friend let him borrow it. Benjamin studied the watch and eventually built his own full-size clock—the first built in America.

News of Benjamin's clock spread throughout Maryland, and he was approached by George Ellicott, a landowner and amateur astronomer. The two became friends, and George lent Benjamin some of his astronomy equipment and books. Benjamin became obsessed with the stars, lying down outside all night to observe the skies, then going to sleep after dawn. When people saw him in bed during the day, they thought he was lazy! As his knowledge grew, Benjamin even spotted errors in George's books.

Around 1791, Benjamin wrote an ephemeris, a chart of the movements of stars and planets. George's cousin Andrew read it and asked Benjamin to be his assistant for a very special project: surveying and designing land that would become Washington, DC, the young nation's new capital. Benjamin agreed, and they set to work.

When his project with Andrew was over, Benjamin returned home and worked on an almanac, a book about upcoming natural events. He used his writing to speak out about the injustice of slavery and defend the humanity and intelligence of black people.

Benjamin was an exceptional scientist and inventor who, through quiet observation and diligent work, helped shape American history.

James Armistead Lafayette
Circa 1748–1830

REVOLUTIONARY WAR SPY

Not much is known about James's life before the Revolutionary War. He was born enslaved in Virginia, and his owner, who managed military supplies, taught James to read and write so he could be a better worker.

During the war against the British, James heard that any slave who fought for the Americans' Continental Army would be freed if the Americans won the war. He got his owner's permission to enlist and in 1781 was assigned to serve under Marquis de Lafayette, a young French aristocrat fighting for the American cause. At first, James used his knowledge of the Virginian landscape to transport messages, but then James and Lafayette had a better idea: James could spy on the British.

Posing as a runaway slave, James went to the British camp commanded by Lord Charles Cornwallis. James helped lead troops through the unfamiliar land. No one suspected that he could read and write, so generals and other soldiers talked about their tactics in front of him and he was given access to British maps and plans. Secretly, he memorized details and reported back to Lafayette. James became so trusted by the British that he was asked to spy on the Americans! He agreed, but gave the British only false information. Equipped with James's accurate information about British troop size, strategies, and morale, the Continental Army defeated the British at Yorktown, effectively ending the war. Imagine Cornwallis's surprise when he entered Lafayette's headquarters to surrender and saw James there!

After the war, enslaved people who served as soldiers were freed. But James had not technically been a soldier, and he was not freed. He petitioned for his release but was ignored. It wasn't until Lafayette wrote a letter commending James's service that his petition was granted and he was freed in 1787. James took the name Lafayette to honor his commander and friend. He lived the rest of his life as a farmer and family man, secretly one of America's greatest heroes.

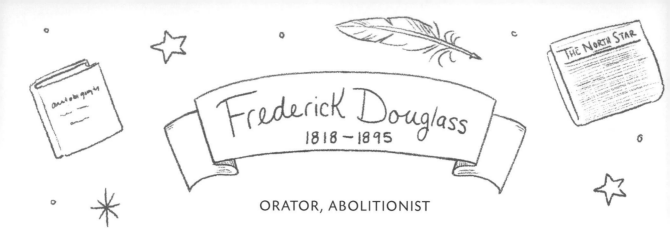

Frederick Douglass
1818 – 1895

ORATOR, ABOLITIONIST

Born enslaved on a plantation in Maryland, Frederick was separated from his mother as an infant. He understood that he was seen and treated as property. When he was eight years old, he was sent to work for Hugh Auld, whose wife taught Frederick how to read. It was illegal for a black person to read and write, a tactic used to keep the enslaved from advancing. When Hugh found out, he put a stop to their lessons, but Frederick had learned enough to be able to teach himself. One of the first books he owned was a collection of historical speeches. So as he learned to read, he was also learning how to give speeches and form an argument, something he would become famous for.

As a devout Christian, Frederick didn't understand how slave owners could co-opt the Gospel to reinforce ideas of slavery. He tried to escape many times and even tried to forge travel papers. He was found out, labeled a troublemaker, and tortured for it. In 1838, he finally made his escape north.

While free, he fought to abolish slavery. In 1841, he spoke at an anti-slavery convention. People were riveted by his eloquence. Northerners didn't understand the experiences of the enslaved, so Frederick published his autobiography, *Narrative of the Life of Frederick Douglass, an American Slave.* It became a bestseller. Some didn't believe he wrote it or experienced it, so he wrote a second one, this time naming his slave owners. It was a risky move, and he had to go to the United Kingdom to avoid recapture. There, he gave speeches, and two of his supporters negotiated to purchase his freedom back in the United States.

He published several anti-slavery newspapers, including the *North Star*. He took his words of abolition to President Lincoln, advocating for the rights of black Union soldiers in the Civil War. He also supported women's suffrage. Frederick's lifelong efforts led to the ratification of the Thirteenth, Fourteenth, and Fifteenth Amendments to the Constitution, and he is remembered as one of the most important people in world history.

Bass Reeves
1838–1910

DEPUTY US MARSHAL

Bass was born enslaved in Arkansas. As a boy, he was made a personal servant to Colonel George Reeves, who allowed Bass to learn to use a shotgun. Bass was so skilled that he even excelled in turkey-shooting competitions. When people saw how good he was, they barred him from competing. Bass understood that, as an enslaved person, there was no winning for him.

George took Bass with him to fight for the Confederacy in the Civil War. Bass was able to escape to Indian Territory—present-day Oklahoma. He hid until the end of the war, learning the languages and customs of the Seminole, Cherokee, and Creek peoples.

It really was the Wild West, a lawless land for miles around. Since tribal courts had no jurisdiction over US citizens, many criminals crossed into Indian Territory to hide out. It was the job of the US marshals to go in and capture the bad guys. In 1875, when the head of the marshals needed to appoint his deputies, he thought of Bass, who knew the land, spoke the languages, and was an incredible shot. Bass was one of the first black deputy US marshals.

It was a dangerous job. In Bass's time, more than a hundred marshals were killed in the line of duty. He was never shot but had a few close calls, including one when the bad guys got his hat! He brought in around three thousand criminals. Before long, people far and wide knew Bass's reputation: the tough-as-nails, sharpshooting, six-foot-two black deputy. He could shoot with both hands, but Bass chose to shoot only when necessary. Instead, he liked to use disguises and tricks to outsmart the criminals to make an arrest. It wasn't just about bad guys for Bass; he loved animals and went out of his way to stand up against animal cruelty.

It's speculated that Bass was the inspiration for the Lone Ranger—the fictional masked hero of the Old West. There's no way of knowing for sure, but we do know that Bass was a real-life good guy who fought for justice.

Robert Smalls
1839–1915

SEAMAN, CONGRESSMAN

Born enslaved in South Carolina, Robert was the son of a black woman and a white man. Because his father was likely one of the white men on the plantation, as a child Robert was given special treatment and was allowed to work on the waterfront in Beaufort. However, his mother made sure to educate her son about the dangers a black person faced in the pro-slavery South.

Robert excelled on the water. Eventually he earned the position of wheelman, effectively the boat's pilot and the highest job a black person could get on a ship. At seventeen, Robert fell in love with an enslaved hotel maid named Hannah. He wanted to purchase her freedom but would never be able to make enough money. To stay together, they needed to escape.

Because he had been sailing for many years when the Civil War began, Robert knew the Charleston waterways well. In 1862, while working aboard the *Planter*, transporting weapons and supplies for the Confederate army, he saw his opportunity to make an escape. When the white officers left the boat for the night, Robert put on a big hat and gloves so that soldiers would think he was the captain. Quietly, the black crew picked up their families and some other enslaved people and set sail north, carefully navigating past the Confederate forts. When they reached the Union blockade, they flew a white flag and Robert surrendered the ship, along with all the Confederate supplies on board. Robert became a national hero and celebrity! He even met with Abraham Lincoln and recruited for the Union navy and army until the end of the war. Afterward, he didn't stop fighting. He moved back to South Carolina, opened a school, and started a newspaper for black people. His record as a war hero helped him become a delegate at the postwar constitutional convention in South Carolina. And in 1874, he was elected to the US House of Representatives.

Robert was a daring and determined man who fought for his country, his people, and his freedom.

Charles Henry Turner
1867 – 1923

ZOOLOGIST, EDUCATOR

As a boy, Charles loved bugs. He would spend his days either outside—observing insects and animals—or indoors, reading from his parents' massive library. His mother had been enslaved and instilled in her son the belief that education would lead to a better life.

Charles graduated from high school as his class valedictorian and studied biology in college. At the University of Cincinnati, he published studies on birds' brains and invertebrates, becoming the first African American to publish in *Science* and the *Journal of Animal Behavior*. Later, he was the first black person to get a PhD in zoology at the University of Chicago.

Throughout his career, Charles struggled—likely because of race—to find steady work at a college or university where he could conduct his research. He committed himself to fighting for civil rights and advocating for black students to have a good education. He even dreamed of starting his own school for black children. While he never did, he eventually settled in St. Louis and taught at the historic black Sumner High School.

Even though Charles didn't have access to the expensive tools and state-of-the-art laboratories that other scientists had, he still developed research methods to make many amazing discoveries about insects. He conducted experiments and determined that bees can see in color. By building mazes, he observed that cockroaches and caterpillars learn by trial and error. He found that ants use light and landmarks to navigate. And he showed that insects have memories and they alter their behavior based on what they remember. Charles also was the first to notice that ants walk around their nest before entering. This action was later named Turner's circling in his honor. By the end of his life, he had published more than seventy research papers and changed the way people viewed insects.

Charles valued hard work and knowledge. A pioneer of comparative research, he led by example and forever broadened our understanding of different behaviors in nature.

Arturo Schomburg
1874–1938

HISTORIAN

When Arturo was growing up in Puerto Rico, he asked his teacher why there weren't any black people in their history books. She told him it was because black people had no history. Even though he was just a kid, Arturo knew this could not be true. He dedicated his life to searching for, collecting, and preserving the stories of Africans around the world.

Arturo began to research on his own, finding stories of people like poet Phillis Wheatley and inventor Benjamin Banneker. Arturo was amazed by the black man who built the first clock in America. Why were there no monuments to him? he wondered. This was the beginning of his quest to find more stories of black heritage.

In 1891, Arturo moved to New York City, where he worked as a law clerk. His main job was to index and organize paperwork—skills that would soon come in handy. In the United States, he was able to pursue his new passion of rare-book hunting. The books he was looking for, written about or by black people, were often really inexpensive. Arturo saw them for what they were: treasures.

Soon his collection grew into a library so big that there was no space left in Arturo's house. In 1926, he sold the entire collection to the New York Public Library for $10,000. Its new home was at the 135th Street branch in Harlem. He used the money to travel to Europe, where he was thrilled to look for art featuring black people.

Arturo dedicated his life to preserving his people's culture, campaigning for Puerto Rican liberation and advocating for black history courses to be included in the US educational system. In 1972, the New York Public Library transferred his collection to a facility that would eventually become the Schomburg Center for Research in Black Culture.

Arturo turned a simple question into a hobby, which grew into a passion, which transformed the way we document cultural history in America. Without his curiosity and excitement, so much history may have been lost to the world forever.

INVENTOR

Garrett was always interested in how things worked. He had no schooling past grade school, but he didn't let that hold him back. By the age of fourteen, he had worked as a handyman, and by eighteen, he had taught himself enough to get jobs at sewing machine companies around Cleveland. In 1901, Garrett sold his first invention (a part for a sewing machine), and a few years later, he was able to open up his own shop! He soon became a successful businessman and inventor.

In 1914, Garrett filed a patent for his next invention. After witnessing a fire, he noticed that the firefighters combated the blazes with no protection over their eyes or face. He thought that a mask could shield the men and keep them from inhaling smoke. He devised a safety hood that covered the face, using a hose to access fresh air from below.

Many people were reluctant to buy inventions made by a black man, so he often hired white actors to conduct demonstrations so customers would give his creations a chance. Eventually, his business grew, and fire departments in Ohio, Pennsylvania, and New York were using his hood! Garrett wasn't just an inventor and businessman, though—he was also a hero. After a tunnel explosion in 1916, Garrett, using his safety hood, rushed in to pull out workers. He saved two lives!

In 1923, he filed a patent for his next invention. At the time, automobiles were on the rise and were sharing the road with horse-drawn carriages, bicycles, and pedestrians. Traffic signals went from STOP to GO with no notice, and it was dangerous. After Garrett witnessed a terrible crash, he had an idea for a warning signal. This was a precursor to the red, yellow, and green signals used today!

Garrett paid attention to the world around him and looked for opportunities everywhere. He proved that inventing wasn't just about coming up with new ideas but could also be about improving upon existing ideas, helping people, and making the world a safer place.

BREATHING DEVICE

Fig.1   Fig.2   Fig.3

Fig 6.   Fig 7

TRAFFIC SIGNAL

Fig 4

INVENTOR
Garrett A. Morgan

Marshall "Major" Taylor
1878–1932

CYCLIST

Born in Indianapolis, Marshall received his first bicycle when he was twelve years old. He practiced his riding skills while delivering newspapers. By 1892, he was so good at doing tricks that he was hired by a local shop to perform stunts outside to draw in customers. He often wore a soldier's uniform as a costume and earned the nickname Major. The shop owner entered Major in a race when he was fourteen—and he won! While he was still an amateur, Major drew lots of attention, including from the former racer Louis Munger, who decided to train him because it was clear: Major was fast.

Cycling was the biggest sport in America, but, like everything else during the Jim Crow era, the industry was incredibly racist. Major was regularly barred from competing. Many were entertained by his skills. Others were not so thrilled. He was often harassed on and off the track, just for being there and being black.

In 1896, he participated in the Six Day Race, a grueling event in which twenty-eight competitors biked as many laps as they could in six days. It was a test of endurance, strength, and will. Major was the only African American. He finished in eighth place—no easy feat. He rode 1,732 miles in 142 hours—roughly the distance from New York to Texas.

This launched Major into the cycling spotlight. In 1899, he competed in the World Championships in Montreal, where he won the one-mile sprint! He was the first African American to win a world championship in cycling and only the second black athlete after the Canadian boxer George Dixon to win a world championship in any sport! For a period, Major held seven world records.

His career was a difficult one, with speed bumps at every turn. But Major blazed a trail wherever he went, and today many cycling groups around the world celebrate his legacy. In 1989, he was posthumously inducted into the US Bicycling Hall of Fame and remembered for the pioneer that he was.

Harold Moody
1882–1947

DOCTOR, PREACHER, LOBBYIST FOR SOCIAL REFORM

Born in Kingston, Jamaica, Harold was considered a British citizen, like all of the Caribbeans under British rule at the time, so he was excited when he was admitted to King's College London in 1904 to study medicine.

However, in London, where few black people lived, he encountered harsh racism. White Londoners would stare and yell at black people on the street, and some black people were even exhibited in the manner of zoo animals. Harold was denied housing many times, and after he graduated, he was refused one hospital post because the matron did not want a black man working there. Instead, he opened his own practice. When he married Olive Tranter, a white nurse, she was told she was a traitor to her race.

Harold didn't think this was right and started to push back—in his quiet, persistent way—against what was known at the time as the "color bar." He opened his house to other black immigrants who needed a place to stay, a job, or a community. He was also in demand as a preacher and challenged congregations that were mostly white to fight against prejudice, but as hard as Harold tried, they couldn't imagine or empathize with black people's experience.

Harold realized that he needed a more proactive way of making change, so he formed the League of Coloured Peoples (LCP), an organization that would lobby the government and companies to improve their policies toward black people. Other activists at the time thought that Harold was too polite, but his method helped open doors. The LCP lobbied for hospitals to hire more black nurses, for changes to be made in how textbooks depicted black people, and for an end to housing discrimination. During World War II, the organization demanded equal treatment for black soldiers and sailors. The league also successfully lobbied for reforms in how the United Kingdom governed its Caribbean colonies.

Harold was a visionary who, as a preacher, doctor, and lobbyist for justice, worked toward a Britain where race didn't hold people back and everyone received a fair chance.

FILMMAKER

Oscar grew up on a farm in Metropolis, Illinois, the fifth of thirteen children. Although he wasn't good at farming, Oscar was a natural salesman, bringing home more money than his siblings for the farm's produce. In school, Oscar was inquisitive and talkative, a little rebellious, and determined to become successful.

At seventeen, he moved to Chicago and did odd jobs until he got a railroad job and traveled across the nation. He saved money and in 1905 bought farmland in South Dakota. Oscar's lack of skill as a farmer resurfaced, but he kept working, and by 1910, he had expanded his farm to five hundred acres.

He wrote several newspaper articles and then a book, *The Conquest*, about being a homesteader in South Dakota, encouraging black people to leave the rural South and urban North and become farmers. Oscar sold his book door-to-door, making enough money to start his own publishing house, Western Book Supply Company.

His third book, *The Homesteader,* caught the attention of the first all-black film company, which made shorts. The producers wanted to adapt his book into a movie. But when Oscar wanted to direct it, they refused. So Oscar turned his publishing company into a production company and made it himself—the first feature-length film by a black person.

In thirty years, Oscar made forty-four movies. He never had a big budget for his films, but he didn't let that stop him. He set up the lights and cameras quickly and filmed only one take of each scene. Once, when he had a meeting with a client who showed up in a fancy coat, Oscar took the coat and excused himself as if to hang it up, but then filmed his actress in the coat before hanging it up and going back to his meeting.

Oscar's films depicted black people as complex human beings, unlike Hollywood films at the time, which typically cast them in the roles of servants or dancers, if they were present at all. Despite all the limitations he faced, Oscar never stopped working to achieve his goals.

Paul Robeson
1898 – 1976

SINGER, ACTOR, ACTIVIST

Paul was good at a lot of things. In school, he engaged in debate and public speaking, and he sang, acted in plays, and played nearly every sport. Despite his talents, he endured constant racism living in pre–civil rights New Jersey. His father, a Presbyterian minister who was born enslaved, instilled in Paul a drive to succeed despite the prejudices of the world around him.

Paul was accepted to Rutgers University on an academic scholarship. He was also a fantastic athlete and achieved celebrity as an all-American football star. While Paul could have pursued football as his main career, he set his sights on law school.

In 1923, Paul graduated from Columbia Law School. He secured a job at a white law firm but was received with racial hostility from clients and colleagues, so he soon left. He had performed in plays all through school, so he turned to acting full-time, eventually starring in Shakespeare's *Othello*. When Broadway writers and producers were creating a multiracial musical called *Show Boat*, they wrote a part for Paul. Unfortunately, he was unable to take part in that production, but he played the role in London in 1928, in the 1932 Broadway revival, and in the 1936 movie. His rendition of the song "Ol' Man River" is legendary.

Paul's acting and singing took him all over the world, and he saw how different race relations were in Europe and the Soviet Union. Paul developed strong leftist beliefs, aligning with the Communist Party. He campaigned for workers' rights and organized for labor and peace. He became a leading activist and helped mentor others, including Claudia Jones and Harry Belafonte. Communism was labeled un-American, however, and in 1950 the State Department barred him from leaving the country, in an attempt to silence him. Paul was blacklisted in the entertainment industry, and his career was ruined.

All-American football star, academic, lawyer, actor, singer, civil rights activist—Paul did it all. And even when he wasn't celebrated for his efforts, Paul continued to advocate for equality and peace.

Aaron Douglas
1899–1979

PAINTER, ILLUSTRATOR

Aaron always knew he wanted to be an artist. As a kid, he liked to follow along with his mother as she drew and painted in watercolors. By the time he was a teen, he was commended as one of the best artists in his school. His journey in art, however, was never easy.

At seventeen, he worked long hours in a machine factory to earn money for college. Then World War I began. Aaron put off graduating to enlist, but at first he was rejected because of his race. His experiences with war, grueling labor, and discrimination stuck with him his whole life, and later they became prominent themes in his paintings.

After college, Aaron read a magazine article about a new artistic scene blossoming in New York City that would soon come to be known as the Harlem Renaissance. The cover illustration by Winold Reiss showed a dignified portrait of a famous African American actor. This thoughtful depiction inspired Aaron so much that he knew he needed to move to New York and create art for and about black people.

In Harlem, Aaron joined the community of writers and artists that included Zora Neale Hurston, Augusta Savage, and Langston Hughes, and he studied painting under Winold. He developed an iconic graphic style influenced by Cubism, Art Deco, and Egyptian art that challenged stereotypes of African Americans with figures that were bold and powerful. His work appeared on book covers and in journals, and in 1925, he illustrated *The New Negro*, Alain Locke's defining book of the moment, which solidified Aaron as the leading artist of the Harlem Renaissance.

Perhaps his most significant works were his large-scale murals, like the four-part masterpiece *Aspects of Negro Life* commissioned by the New York Public Library. Aaron filled these colorful paintings with stories, symbols, meaning, and beauty. He created art that he hoped would foster a strong sense of racial pride. He continued that idea in his teaching career, founding the art department at Fisk University.

Louis Armstrong
1901 – 1971

JAZZ MUSICIAN

Louis was born in the same place as jazz—New Orleans. He had a rough upbringing, living in a neighborhood so dangerous it was nicknamed the Battlefield. He got his first job at age seven, collecting scrap around town. Riding through the streets, he played a small tin horn and soon realized that he could play a whole song. Louis saved up enough money to buy a nice cornet to continue practicing.

Trouble was not far away, however. At a 1912 New Year's Eve celebration, Louis was arrested for firing off a pistol. He was sent to a home for troubled boys. Amazingly, the home had a band—brass bands have been an integral part of New Orleans culture since the late 1800s—and Louis was given real cornet lessons. The band marched to his neighborhood, and his friends and family couldn't believe that was Louis playing for real. It was the first major step in his musical journey.

At eleven, he performed on the streets with a vocal quartet. They caught the attention of a local cornetist, King Oliver, who was keen to advise Louis on technique and skill. By 1918, Louis was performing enough to make a living, playing in the most popular band in town. In 1922, King invited him to Chicago, where, with his strong New Orleans–influenced sound, Louis flourished. From 1925 to 1928, he recorded his first records with his own band. They were some of the most influential records in jazz history. He became famous for his improvised solos, unmistakable vocals, and scatting.

Louis had many hit recordings, including "La Vie en Rose" and "What a Wonderful World." Over the years, he received criticism from younger jazz musicians for his old-fashioned stage persona and his silence on politics, but throughout his career, he broke down barriers and took a stand for civil rights. He's had many nicknames, including Satchmo and Pops, but the moniker Ambassador Satch he earned for his dedication to sharing jazz all over the world.

POET

Langston moved around a lot as a child. His parents traveled looking for work—his father to Mexico and his mother throughout the Midwest. Langston was left to be raised by his grandmother but felt abandoned by his parents. His only comforts were his books and the worlds he found inside them.

Langston began writing early. In the eighth grade, he was made class poet, and his first works were printed in his school's newspaper. In 1920, he went to visit his father. As the train crossed the Mississippi, he thought about the massive river, how black history was linked to it. He thought about things his grandmother had told him, things he'd read in books about the slave trade, and he crafted one of his first major poems, "The Negro Speaks of Rivers." He was only seventeen, but his voice had the wisdom of someone who saw the world for what it was. He asked the reader to consider humanity, not just black or white society.

In 1921, the poem was published in the *Crisis,* a major publication of the Harlem Renaissance. Langston moved to New York to attend Columbia University and became a leading creative voice in the movement. Langston wrote about black pride at a time long before anyone considered it something to celebrate. Heavily influenced by the blues and jazz, his poetry flowed and had rhythm.

In 1923, he traveled abroad, settling for a while in Paris. Upon his return, he worked as a busboy in Washington, DC. One day, one of his favorite writers, Vachel Lindsay, came in, and Langston slipped him some of his work. Vachel was impressed with Langston's poetry and helped him meet the right people. In 1926, Langston's first book of poems was published: *The Weary Blues.*

He was the first black writer in the United States to make a living off his work. He wrote plays and published short stories and more than sixteen volumes of poems. Langston used his writing to appeal to working-class folks, focus on society and racial injustice, and portray black life in America.

Charles R. Drew
1904–1950

SURGEON

Although he was a bright student, Charles didn't have perfect grades or always know exactly what he wanted to do. Two experiences got him interested in medicine: an injury on the football field and his sister's tuberculosis. Afterward, he became passionate about medicine and understanding how the body worked. He went to Montreal to study at the McGill University Faculty of Medicine. The Canadian school had a better reputation than most in the United States for its treatment of minority students. He graduated second in his class of 137.

During his surgical residency, working with bacteriologist John Beattie, Charles became interested in transfusion medicine: the transference of blood and blood products. Through his research, Charles found that if you separate the blood from the plasma (the liquid portion of blood without the blood cells), it could last much longer—making it possible for blood to be stored. It could be preserved and shipped overseas, even taken out onto the battlefield. In 1940, after Britain was attacked by Nazi Germany, Charles was asked to lead a special medical effort called Blood for Britain.

Months before the United States entered World War II, Charles became assistant director of a new national blood banking system for the American Red Cross. They collected more than ten thousand pints of blood for the war effort. The military, however, decreed that blood taken from African American donors had to be segregated from whites' blood and couldn't be transfused into them. Blood has no racial characteristics, so Charles knew this was wrong, both scientifically and morally. He spoke up, and in 1941, he resigned from his job. He returned to his former employer, Howard University, and became chief of surgery at its Freedmen's Hospital. He spent the next nine years mentoring students and advocating for the education and inclusion of African Americans in medicine.

Charles's discoveries were responsible for countless lives being saved and transformed the medical field forever. He was a pioneer who took a stand for what was right.

John Robinson
Circa 1905–1954

AVIATOR

When John was a young boy, he saw something amazing: a new invention that burst through the clouds and landed in front of him in the blue waters of Gulfport, Mississippi. People gathered to catch a glimpse of the flying machine—including John and his mother. They called it an aeroplane. Like most people in Mississippi, John had never seen one before, but from that day on, he dreamed of becoming a pilot.

When he was old enough, John enrolled at the Tuskegee Institute in Alabama to study mechanical repair, then applied to the Curtiss-Wright Aeronautical University. However, the school didn't allow black students. That didn't stop John. He got a job as a janitor, sitting in on classes and reading the papers students threw away. Along with friend and fellow airman Cornelius Coffey, he formed the Challenger Air Pilots Association for other black people interested in aviation. Together, they built their own airplane. One of the Curtiss-Wright instructors was so impressed that he invited John to attend the school!

After graduating in 1931, John began teaching at Curtiss-Wright. He later started a flight school to train black pilots. In 1934, he returned to Tuskegee to get students excited about aviation. His efforts led to the formation of the Tuskegee Airmen, the first all-black group of pilots in the US Air Force.

John believed that black people should help other black people no matter where they were from, so in 1935, when Italy invaded Ethiopia, John volunteered to join the Ethiopian army and build its air force. His planes lacked weapons, so John flew reconnaissance and supply missions while training pilots. John's adventures were reported internationally, and he was dubbed the Brown Condor of Ethiopia.

Many people know of the Tuskegee Airmen and their landmark role in World War II, but if it were not for John and his perseverance, the aviation program might never have existed. Even though few know his name, his legacy has helped influence American and world history forever.

Thurgood Marshall
1908–1993

SUPREME COURT JUSTICE

Thoroughgood (later shortened to Thurgood) was a naturally argumentative boy and a bit of a troublemaker. His punishment for talking too much was to memorize the US Constitution. Which was probably not the worst thing for him, considering that one day he would become one of the world's leading constitutional scholars.

By the time he applied to college, Thurgood knew he wanted to be a lawyer. He hoped to attend the University of Maryland (UMD) School of Law but couldn't because he was black. The anger and frustration about that instilled in him a deep desire for justice and equality. Instead, he earned his law degree from the historically black college Howard University.

Not long after graduation in 1933, Thurgood began working with his mentor, Charles Houston, for the NAACP. He wanted to help fight for civil rights. Their major goal was to overturn the US Supreme Court ruling that segregation was legal if the segregated facilities were "separate but equal." Black people in America knew that their facilities were nowhere near equal and that they had nothing close to the same opportunities as white people. Thurgood had proof: UMD School of Law. He and Charles made the case to Maryland state courts that in order to uphold the separate-but-equal law, UMD would need to have a second school that admitted black students. In 1936, they won! It was the first in a long line of cases they brought to take down legal segregation. Then, in 1954, Thurgood brought the case of *Brown v. Board of Education of Topeka* to the US Supreme Court. It was the landmark ruling that would lead to the end of legal segregation in the country!

In 1967, Thurgood was appointed as an associate justice to the US Supreme Court—he would be the first African American justice. In his long career, he was well known for his constitutional knowledge and even helped the United Nations draft the constitutions for the newly formed countries Ghana and present-day Tanzania. Thurgood spent so much of his life fighting for justice; it was a long road but he never lost hope.

Gordon Parks
1912–2006

PHOTOGRAPHER

Growing up poor and black in Kansas, the youngest of fifteen children, Gordon had to be clever to get by. When he was fifteen, his mother died, and Gordon was sent to live with his older sister. Her husband didn't like kids and quickly kicked Gordon out. Homeless but undeterred, Gordon continued to attend school and rode train cars at night to stay warm.

During the Great Depression, while working as a waiter aboard a train, Gordon picked up a magazine one day and saw photos of migrant workers. The images touched him. He studied them for weeks. Later, impressed by the heroism of a war photographer he'd met, Gordon decided to become a photographer so that he could capture and share the realities of the world he had seen and experienced.

He taught himself photography. He eventually earned a fellowship taking pictures for the federal Farm Security Administration, documenting poverty and discrimination, such as in *American Gothic,* one of his most renowned photos. For years, he both chronicled American life and shot fashion photography, using his charisma and empathy to connect with his subjects. In 1948, *Life* magazine hired him—the first black photographer on staff.

Gordon felt fortunate because of his success and wanted to help others, so he started writing books, first about photography, then about his life. His 1964 semi-autobiographical novel, *The Learning Tree,* was a huge smash, and he was approached to make a movie based on it. As always, Gordon leaped at the chance. He wrote, directed, produced, and scored *The Learning Tree*, becoming the first black director to work in Hollywood.

Over the years, Gordon wrote books, directed films, composed music, and even created a ballet in honor of Martin Luther King Jr. He not only shined a light on the African American experience but also made a lasting impact on history, art, and fashion in America. He saw challenges as opportunities and used his unique vision and masterly skills to share his life and the lives of others with the world.

Jacob Lawrence
1917–2000

PAINTER

Jacob and his mother arrived in the Harlem neighborhood of New York City in 1930. They were part of a historic migration of black Americans, moving from the South to the North in search of opportunities, stable jobs, and better living conditions. In the North, there were opportunities for black people even in the arts. Sensing her thirteen-year-old son's energy and creativity, Jacob's mother enrolled him in an after-school art program. He was already so skillful that his instructors just wanted to let him paint.

Jacob is often associated with the Harlem Renaissance, but in its closing years, he was still a kid. Although he was not a part of the movement's group of artists and thinkers, some of them were his teachers. Charles Alston and Augusta Savage mentored him in art, and historian Charles Seifert encouraged him to explore black history.

Jacob combined his graphic and modern painting style with his newfound appreciation for history and began a series of biographical works. In 1938, at the age of twenty-one, he finished his first notable collection: a forty-one-piece series chronicling the life and accomplishments of the Haitian leader Toussaint L'Ouverture.

At a time before black history was widely celebrated, Jacob made a conscious effort to bring the name of Toussaint into the mainstream. He went on to paint other historic figures, including Harriet Tubman and Frederick Douglass. His most famous work was a series recounting the African American journey from the South to the North, like the experience he and his mother had gone through. *The Migration Series* was a sixty-panel masterpiece that catapulted Jacob into the artistic spotlight.

Jacob didn't love all the attention. He felt guilty that he eclipsed his mentors, like Augusta and Charles, and dedicated the rest of his life to making art and mentoring young artists. He is remembered for his use of art to examine and capture the experiences of African Americans and their everyday struggles.

Ousmane Sembène
1923–2007

FILMMAKER

Who would have guessed that this son of a fisherman would one day become known as the father of African cinema? Raised in Senegal by his grandmother, an oral storyteller, Ousmane developed a love for stories early on. His journey to filmmaking, though, would take him to several different countries over many years.

Ousmane began working at a young age, doing hard labor as a bricklayer and dockworker. He witnessed firsthand the struggles of his people. Participating in a union strike, he saw the impact an educated and united group could have on a powerful institution, something he would bring to his filmmaking.

In 1947, while working as a labor organizer and longshoreman in France, Ousmane broke his back carrying a heavy load. As he recovered, he spent long hours in the library, where he found revolutionary writers and thinkers from around the globe—except for Africa. Ousmane decided he needed to share the stories of Africans, so he started writing.

He published several books depicting the lives of Senegalese people, revealing corruption in the government, and calling for social change. But as Ousmane traveled through West Africa, he noticed that although many people did not read, they did go to the movies, so he decided to switch to filmmaking.

He hit the ground running with his first feature, *La noire de...* (1966), which debuted at the Cannes Film Festival, one of the top festivals in the world. His next film, *Mandabi* (1968), was the first movie in the indigenous Wolof language instead of French, which was dominant in pre-1960 colonial Senegal. Ousmane's films angered those in power, but he wanted to get their attention by speaking up for regular people. Despite his films being censored in his country, Ousmane stayed true to his beliefs and vision, creating a uniquely African style of filmmaking inspired by oral storytelling. He put African film on the map and is celebrated around the world for giving a voice to the people and cultures of the continent.

James Baldwin
1924–1987

WRITER, ACTIVIST

When he was fourteen, James thought he would become a minister like his stepfather. James was already a great orator, giving sermons in front of congregations. However, he felt frustrated with the church. Around that time, James realized he was gay. The systemic racism and homophobia coming from an institution that was supposed to share messages of grace and love made him feel lost, disappointed, and alone. James left the church and focused on developing his writing skills.

For a while, he worked odd jobs and was mentored by writers like Richard Wright and Countee Cullen. Eventually, James felt suffocated by racism and left the country. In 1948, he went to Paris, where he could live and work without fear. In 1953, he published his first novel, *Go Tell It on the Mountain*, inspired by his experiences with religion, class, and exile.

In the United States, the Civil Rights Movement was blossoming, and James wanted to participate. During this period, his writing focused on what it meant to be black in America. James felt that segregation was the biggest source of strife in the country and that racism hurt white society as well as black. He called for human equality and encouraged brotherhood over violence. At times, he was criticized for his pacifism, but James never had hatred for any people, only for the establishment and institutions that told people what to do.

He became well known for articulating arguments in an elegant way that made black and white audiences listen. He traveled the country, giving speeches and lectures, and he debated and befriended some of the biggest leaders of the day.

Many of James's essays, poems, and novels are considered masterpieces, including *Notes of a Native Son* and *The Fire Next Time*. He wrote openly about his sexuality at a time when no one else did. For all his work and his words, James was watched closely by the Federal Bureau of Investigation (FBI), perhaps because the agency knew the power he had to galvanize the people around him with his sharp and bold messages.

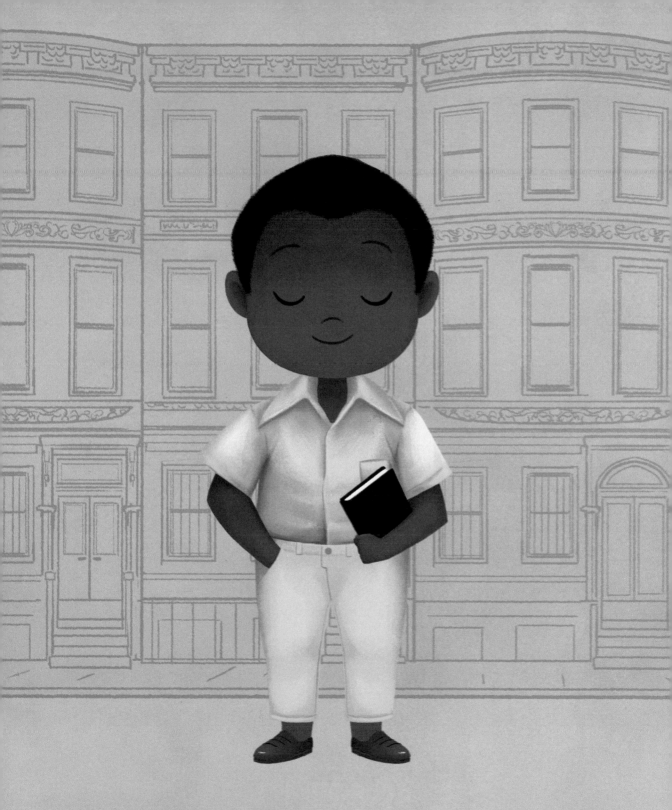

Harry Belafonte
1927–

SINGER, ACTOR, ACTIVIST

Harry was born in Harlem but spent much of his childhood on the island of Jamaica, where his mother was from. In New York City, he and his immigrant parents lived with other families from around the world. Harry always remembered how hard each family worked, how little they earned, and how much they supported one another.

School was difficult and Harry felt that he didn't fit in, so he dropped out at seventeen and joined the US Navy. (Later, Harry discovered that he was dyslexic, which explained why school was such a challenge for him.) Afterward, it was by chance that he found his calling: While he was working as a janitor, he received as a tip tickets to a play. Harry had never been to a play before and fell in love with the theater. He took acting classes and started auditioning, but when he landed a job at a nightclub singing popular songs, he found success.

As his career grew, Harry chose to stop singing familiar hits and instead sang the Caribbean folk songs he had heard growing up, such as "The Banana Boat Song (Day-O)" and "Jump in the Line." Americans hadn't heard anything like this music, and Harry became a singing sensation, known as the King of Calypso.

Throughout his career, Harry received numerous awards—for his performances as well as for his humanitarian work. He never took any roles that demeaned black people, and later he created his own film production company, which made movies that defied stereotypes of blackness. Harry gave a voice to underrepresented cultures and altered the image of black people in the media.

Harry worked with his friend Martin Luther King Jr. and fought for civil rights, marching and protesting as well as encouraging other celebrities to participate. He even helped organize the 1963 March on Washington for Jobs and Freedom. Harry used his talents, popularity, and prestige to help make real change in the world. He encouraged future generations of artists to use their voices for good.

Alvin Ailey
1931 – 1989

CHOREOGRAPHER

Alvin was a quiet kid. While growing up in rural Texas, he and his mother moved from place to place. They always found community, though, in the local black churches and dance halls. In 1943, they moved to Los Angeles, where Alvin was introduced to dance and theater.

When Alvin was in junior high school, he went on a class trip to see the Ballet Russe de Monte Carlo, but it was a performance by Katherine Dunham's company, one of the first black modern dance troupes in America, that sparked his interest in the art form. However, he didn't consider studying dance until he was inspired by a classmate's performance at school. Alvin couldn't believe a boy was dancing!

In 1949, Alvin attended the Lester Horton Dance Theater, America's first integrated dance company. The dancers learned techniques from Native American, Japanese, Caribbean, Javanese, and Balinese traditions. Alvin trained with Horton on and off for a few years. When Horton died suddenly, Alvin took over as the director and lead choreographer, even though he was only twenty-two years old!

In 1954, Alvin moved to New York. The Civil Rights Movement had begun, and Alvin wanted to contribute by sharing his art. He formed the Alvin Ailey American Dance Theater in 1958 and used dance to affirm that black people were a part of American culture. His work during this period recalled his childhood in Texas. *Blues Suite,* his first solo success, drew from a dance hall he had frequented. *Revelations* was based on his experience in the Baptist church and is still performed to this day.

He focused on black dancers and choreographers but included dancers of every race. Nicknamed "American cultural ambassadors to the world," the troupe traveled all over. In 1969, he opened the Alvin Ailey American Dance Center to foster creativity in underserved communities. Alvin helped popularize modern dance internationally and brought more African Americans into the field. He shared his vision of blackness while inspiring dancers everywhere.

Bill Russell
1934–

BASKETBALL PLAYER AND COACH

As a kid, Bill was introverted and awkward. After the untimely death of his mother, Bill and his father and brother had to be a team and stick together. During high school, Bill grew to be six feet five and was recruited onto the basketball court. He wasn't the best player, but he was smart and he paid attention. Watching closely, he mirrored his opponents, blocking shots—which at the time was considered a bad play. But it led to wins and later redefined how defense was played.

Although he was still improving his skills, Bill also worked hard to be the best teammate he could be, listening to his fellow players and adapting his game to support them. As he got better, Bill earned championships in high school and college, and he won a gold medal in the Olympics. In 1956, he joined the Boston Celtics, and in his thirteen years there, the team won eleven championships. In 1966, he became the Celtics' player-coach, coaching while still playing. He was the first black coach in the National Basketball Association (NBA)!

Bill believed that athletes should be idolized not for their abilities on the court but for how they lived their lives. He always stood up for what he thought was right. Bill ran an integrated youth basketball camp in Mississippi while enduring racist taunts and threats by the Ku Klux Klan. Many Bostonians didn't like that Bill was so outspoken and politically active. Some people even broke into his house, spray-painted his walls, and smashed his trophies. When he retired in 1969, Bill vowed never to return to Boston.

In 2009, the NBA named the Finals Most Valuable Player Award after Bill, and he was further honored two years later when he received the Presidential Medal of Freedom from Barack Obama. As time went on, the city of Boston changed and the people realized Bill's importance as a player, coach, and leader. In 2013, a statue of him was unveiled there. During his career, Bill always worked hard. He never compromised his principles; he only waited for the world to catch up.

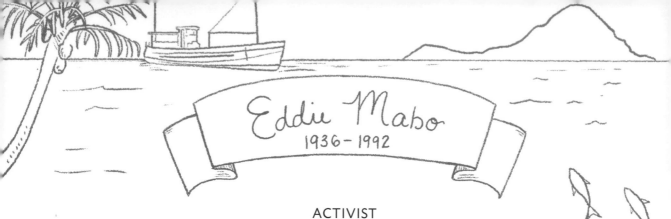

Eddie Mabo
1936–1992

ACTIVIST

Eddie was born on the island of Mer in the Torres Strait, between Australia and Papua New Guinea. The people in his community were native to the islands, and they'd had their own customs, laws, and rituals for generations. Eddie was determined, ambitious, and a little bit rebellious—qualities that made him a great activist, but as a teen they got him exiled from Mer for one year for a small offense. He moved to the state of Queensland in Australia.

When the year was up, he didn't return home. Instead, he traveled, worked odd jobs, and became involved in the indigenous community, developing a fighting spirit. He met his wife, Bonita, and together they worked for indigenous peoples' rights and grew a large family. In 1967, he campaigned to get the right for Aboriginal and island people to vote. In 1973, he and Bonita opened the Black Community School in Townsville to give Aboriginal children a cultural and traditional education. But it was through his job as a groundskeeper at James Cook University that Eddie found a new challenge.

On campus, Eddie befriended many of the professors. During a conversation with some humanities professors, Eddie spoke of his home, and his property, on Mer. The professors were surprised to hear that Eddie believed he owned that land. Eddie was shocked to hear he didn't. In the eighteenth century, when European colonizers first traveled to Australia, they made rules claiming that the area was "terra nullius," or "nobody's land," and could now be the property of the government.

Eddie knew that wasn't right, and he began a legal battle for traditional landownership by his people. The fight took almost ten years. In that time, Eddie's health and spirits diminished, and in January 1992 he passed away. On June 3 in that same year, the High Court of Australia ruled in favor of land rights for the islanders. The landmark ruling is now famously known simply as the Mabo decision. Eddie's work changed the legal and political landscape in Australia forever! June 3 is now celebrated as Mabo Day.

Paul Stephenson
1937 –

ACTIVIST

Despite growing up in the shadow of World War II, Paul had a happy childhood. He was two years old when the war began, and he was evacuated from London to the countryside. Since his mother was in the military and his father had returned to West Africa, he grew up in a children's home. The only black person in town, Paul was treated kindly, but sometimes as a curiosity. Being singled out made him particularly observant about the behaviors of the adults around him, a trait that served him well later in life.

When he moved back to London, Paul experienced racist hostility for the first time. Despite this, Paul was proud to be British and wanted justice for everyone. At fifteen, he joined the Royal Air Force. After seven years of service, he moved to Bristol, where he was the city's first black social worker.

When Paul arrived in Bristol, he witnessed the racism that many Caribbean immigrants were experiencing. The Bristol Omnibus Company, for example, refused to employ black or Asian drivers. Inspired by the work of civil rights activists in the United States like Martin Luther King Jr. and Rosa Parks, Paul called for a bus boycott, which lasted sixty days. On August 28, 1963, the same day Dr. King gave his "I Have a Dream" speech, the bus company announced it would hire black and Asian drivers!

Paul didn't stop there. In 1964, he was refused service at a pub because he was black. In protest, he decided to stay until he was served. He was arrested, and the trial received media attention, forcing Britain to confront its racism. Paul was found innocent, and Britain's prime minister promised him that the laws would change. In 1965, the Race Relations Act was passed, making racial discrimination illegal in public places, and Paul's work helped pave the way for it.

Paul showed that it's important to stand up for what is right, no matter how big or small the fight. He shined a light on Britain's racism and helped illuminate a path to a better country.

John Lewis
1940 –

ACTIVIST, MEMBER OF CONGRESS

People always knew John was meant to be a leader. When he was young, he dreamed of being a minister: Dressed in a shirt and tie, he preached to the chickens on his family's farm. Even at home, though, he was aware of discrimination in segregated Alabama. Nicer schools, libraries, and buses were reserved for white people. John thought this was unfair. His parents told him to leave it alone, but he wanted to make things better.

At around the age of fifteen, John heard Dr. Martin Luther King Jr. on the radio, describing how non-violent protests such as marches and boycotts were helping to end segregation. John was inspired and attended his first march. In college, he wrote to Dr. King, asking for advice on how to do more. Amazingly, Dr. King wrote him back, met with him, and soon became a friend and mentor!

John organized sit-ins and participated in Freedom Rides, where young black and white activists would sit together in segregated diners and buses. By the age of twenty-three, John was one of the "Big Six" civil rights leaders who worked with Dr. King and one another to organize the 1963 March on Washington for Jobs and Freedom.

In 1965, John and six hundred others planned to march from Selma to Montgomery in Alabama. When they crossed the Edmund Pettus Bridge, state troopers were waiting for them. The troopers attacked the protesters, injuring many, including John, whose skull was fractured. The images from the march—of peaceful protesters being beaten—made it onto the national news. Americans were horrified, and this led to a wave of support for civil rights.

Over the years, John has received many honors for fighting for the rights of his fellow Americans. And he's still using non-violence. He has held a seat in the US House of Representatives, serving Atlanta's Fifth District, since 1987. In 2016, he led a sit-in at the US Capitol to push for gun control laws. As a boy, John wanted to change the world, and as a man, he keeps on changing it.

Arthur Ashe
1943–1993

TENNIS PLAYER

Growing up in segregated Richmond, Virginia, a black boy like Arthur was unlikely to play tennis, a historically white sport. Fortunately, his father was the caretaker of a park that had facilities for black people. Young Arthur had a racket in his hands by age six!

As he got older, segregation and other forms of discrimination kept him from regular training, but he met Dr. Robert Walter Johnson, who ran a tennis camp in Lynchburg for black athletes (including women's champion Althea Gibson). Both Dr. Johnson and Arthur's father were disciplined and strict. They taught him to always keep his cool. Black athletes had to live by a high standard because their actions on the court had real-world consequences.

Arthur played in whites-only tournaments and opened up doors for other athletes of color. In 1968, he won the first US Open of the modern era, and in 1975 was the first black male to win Wimbledon. On the tennis court, Arthur was a star, but off the court he was a naturally quiet person.

With the South African Open, Arthur found his opportunity to use his voice. At the time, South Africa practiced a form of segregation known as apartheid, and the government wouldn't let him into the country to compete. Arthur spoke out. He even testified in front of Congress, saying, "Athletes, especially black athletes, must use every resource at their command to right things that are wrong." In 1973, South Africa finally let Arthur enter the country and play in the tournament. Over the years, Arthur continued to use his voice to bring attention to racism around the world.

In the 1980s, Arthur contracted HIV during heart surgery. He kept his diagnosis a secret until 1992, when he used it as an opportunity to speak out for the rights of HIV-positive people, including those like him with full-blown AIDS.

He kept speaking out for underrepresented people until he passed away in 1993. Arthur proved that even a quiet person can be a big voice for change in the world.

Andre Leon Talley
1949–

FASHION EDITOR

André grew up with an appreciation for style. He was raised by his grandmother, a domestic worker, in Durham, North Carolina. Even though they didn't have much, they took care of what they had. With clothes freshly pressed, they went to church every Sunday. Attending a black church in the South was almost like going to a fashion show, and André saw how clothing could make people feel different. With the right outfit, folks in his small town could transform into aristocrats. He found his first copy of *Vogue* magazine at the library and soon had stacks of his own, with pages pinned to his bedroom walls.

He earned a scholarship to attend Brown University, where he studied French literature and befriended art students at the nearby Rhode Island School of Design (RISD). André developed his now iconic sense of style, donning capes and fedoras, and found his creative voice, writing a column for the RISD newspaper.

After graduation, he moved to New York and met his idol, Diana Vreeland, the visionary former editor in chief of *Vogue*. She was heading up the Costume Institute at the Metropolitan Museum of Art. As an intern there, he impressed her so much that she took him under her wing, becoming his mentor and friend.

In 1983, he got his first role at *Vogue*, for which he traveled to fashion shows around the world. Five years later, he became creative director of the magazine, and in 1998 he became editor at large. The fashion industry has historically been dominated by white high society, with *Vogue* magazine as its foremost publication—and for years, André, a six-foot-six black man from North Carolina, was one of its leading voices!

Despite rising in the fashion ranks, André has always stayed grounded. He has actively advocated for diversity in the fashion industry. The people who influenced André the most—his grandmother and Mrs. Vreeland—showed him unconditional love, and that is what he reflects back into the world. André proved that grace and kindness are always in style.

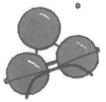

Prince
1958–2016

MUSICIAN

With two musicians for parents, Prince Rogers Nelson grew up in Minneapolis surrounded by music. He began playing piano and wrote his first song at seven! He eventually taught himself to play guitar, bass, and drums.

His parents' divorce when he was twelve years old shook up his home life. To make matters worse, he suffered from epilepsy and was teased at school for being so small. He was shy and insecure, but all of his troubles fell away when he focused on music.

As a teen, Prince started his first band, Grand Central. To counteract his insecurities, he wore flashy clothes and was as loud, wild, and weird as possible when he performed. His music was a mix of funk, disco, rock, rhythm and blues, and gospel. No one had ever heard anything like him before, and producers fought to sign him to a record deal.

In 1979, he started a new band, the Revolution, whose members were black, white, male, and female. When they performed, they all dressed to impress—and sometimes the men wore clothes designed for women and the women wore clothes designed for men. This made some people uncomfortable, but his fans were inspired to do what they wanted and be themselves, no matter what others thought.

Prince and the Revolution made some of the bestselling albums ever, including *Parade, 1999,* and *Purple Rain,* the soundtrack to the movie *Purple Rain,* starring...Prince! In 1984, Prince became one of the few artists with both a number one album and number one movie, and he even won both a Grammy and an Oscar.

Prince liked to change things up all the time, and each change fueled his creativity. He made waves for his bold choices, and he is remembered as much for his flashy style and big personality as for the many songs he wrote. He always tried to help people in his community and even mentored up-and-coming artists. He was a virtuoso musician, composer, and vocalist who will go down in history as one of music's greats.

Chuck D
1960–

RAPPER

Born Carlton Ridenhour, Chuck always had a booming voice. When he was growing up on Long Island, near New York City, his parents enrolled him in a summer course run by former members of the Black Panther Party, a militant political group formed in the 1960s that encouraged black pride. His parents wanted him to learn about his history and use his voice to uplift his people, but at that time he was more interested in bossing around his younger siblings and practicing to be a sportscaster. When Chuck heard a new type of music from the Bronx called rap, he fell in love with it. It would be a while, though, before he combined his voice, his understanding of history, and this music.

Chuck studied graphic design in college and created flyers for local hip-hop shows while DJing with his friends at his school's radio station. When a producer wanted to sign him to Def Jam Records, Chuck thought he was too old. But his age—twenty-six—meant he had a different perspective from the younger rappers coming up.

Eventually, he was convinced and, with his radio show buddies, formed the group Public Enemy. Chuck saw rap as a way to talk about and influence the black community—he called rap "black America's TV station." He rapped about racism, politics, culture, and the importance of unity and uplift.

At first, Public Enemy had a hard time breaking out. Their lyrics were deemed too political to be played on the radio—at a time when you couldn't find success without radio play. But when popular director Spike Lee featured their song "Fight the Power" in his movie *Do the Right Thing* (1989), their audience grew.

In 2013, Public Enemy was inducted into the Rock and Roll Hall of Fame—one of only a handful of rap and hip-hop inductees. Chuck's intelligence and dedication to political and social change have made him a statesman for hip-hop. As both an activist and artist—or, as he has called himself, a "raptivist"—Chuck and his booming voice will be heard for generations to come.

Dwayne McDuffie
1962–2011

COMIC BOOK AUTHOR AND PUBLISHER

As a kid, Dwayne loved two things more than anything else: science and science fiction. He entered as many science fairs as possible and read all the comic books he could get his hands on. He always dreamed of one day bringing his passions together to become an astronaut, but in high school something happened that led him down another path: Just for fun, Dwayne shot a silly film about Batman. Everyone loved it, and Dwayne started to think he could create stories for a living.

He graduated from the University of Michigan with a master's degree in physics, but in 1983, he moved to New York to attend film school. One day, a friend told him about a job at Marvel Comics working on superhero trading cards. Dwayne quickly moved up the ranks at Marvel, writing for such characters as Spider-Man, Captain Marvel, and She-Hulk while creating his own comic called *Damage Control*.

While working in the comics industry, Dwayne noticed that there weren't a lot of characters of color, and the ones he did see didn't seem authentic. Dwayne decided to help make a change. In 1993, Dwayne and other black comic creators formed Milestone Media. There, they could publish their own comics with a range of characters to represent their cultures. They told stories rooted in the issues of the day—racism, violence, poverty—and mixed them with comic book favorites: shape-shifting aliens and giant mutants.

Milestone eventually became the most successful minority-owned comic publisher ever. Its comic *Static Shock* was a huge success and got its own animated television series, with Dwayne as a writer and producer. He was so good that he was invited to write for other animated shows such as *Justice League Unlimited* and *Teen Titans*. Dwayne never forgot his roots, though, and returned to comics to write for the Justice League and Fantastic Four.

Dwayne was a true champion for a more inclusive comic book landscape, and through it all, he entertained and enlightened audiences with fantasy and humor.

Leland Melvin
1964–

ASTRONAUT

Leland didn't grow up wanting to be an astronaut. He watched the moon landing on TV with his family but didn't see anyone who looked like him, so he never even considered wanting that for himself. He did grow up wanting to be like Arthur Ashe, the star athlete who had trained five blocks from where Leland grew up, in Lynchburg, Virginia.

Around the time he started playing sports, he got his first chemistry set and accidentally burned a hole in the carpet! He was amazed at how powerful chemicals could become once they were mixed. While on a football scholarship at the University of Richmond, Leland majored in chemistry. His classmates couldn't believe he was both an academic and an athlete.

After graduation, he was drafted into the National Football League (NFL). Unfortunately, he damaged a hamstring in training camp. It could have been the end of Leland's dreams, but his other love, science, was calling.

Leland got a job at NASA Langley Research Center while earning his master's degree at the University of Virginia. At Langley, a friend suggested that he apply to become an astronaut. He was accepted on his first try! Being a candidate didn't mean he automatically got to go to space, though. He went into training, and again he was injured. He was in the Neutral Buoyancy Lab, a big pool of water meant to simulate the feeling of space, when he suffered ear damage that left him partially deaf—and unfit for spaceflight.

This didn't make him any less of an astronaut. For several years, he worked at the Johnson Space Center in Houston and visited schools to talk about NASA. After some healing, he learned he had been reapproved for flight. In 2008, on the space shuttle *Atlantis*, he flew into space on the twenty-fourth mission to the International Space Station.

Through football, Leland learned perseverance and teamwork, and through his career as a scientist and astronaut, he learned patience and adaptability. In his life, he found that no plan is fixed, but that hard work and dedication allowed him to reach new heights.

Sir David Adjaye
1966–

ARCHITECT

As the son of a Ghanaian diplomat, David lived in many countries throughout his youth. He learned about different cultures and various art forms. After David's youngest brother became paralyzed and began using a wheelchair, the family settled in London to get better medical treatment. David never forgot how his family had to access buildings through ill-conceived and humiliating handicapped entrances.

At school, David excelled in many subjects, but when one of his teachers encouraged him to take an art course, he discovered architecture. David appreciated its power to shape societies and serve communities. After studying at the Royal Academy of Arts, he traveled all over the world, observing how buildings work within their environments. David's designs are noted for his use of patterns, many influenced by his African heritage. The blue and green windows in the Idea Stores in London resemble the bold, geometric woven pattern of kente cloth while also mimicking the awnings that the building overlooks.

David's experience with his brother made him consider the social responsibilities of an architect. His design for the Moscow School of Management SKOLKOVO is made up of four buildings, all connected so that no one should have to go outside during the freezing winters.

With the National Museum of African American History and Culture, which opened in 2016, David was designing more than a building—he was creating an actual monument that sits on the National Mall, not far from the Washington Monument and the Martin Luther King Jr. Memorial. It needed to be a beautiful structure that housed painful memories, but he also wanted it to be a joyous celebration of black history in America, inside and out. He used metal designs influenced by black craftsmen from the American South, while the building's three-level shape was inspired by a Yoruban crown.

In 2017, David was knighted for his services to architecture. He continues to use his curiosity and creativity to make the world a more beautiful—and socially conscious—place.

More Little Legends

Exceptional men are everywhere. When we were brainstorming for this book, the original list was more than one hundred people too long! Sadly, there was no way to fit in everyone whose story deserves to be told, but that is just a testament to all the wonderful things people have done in this world.

It was definitely not easy to craft the full list, so here in the "More Little Legends" section you will find eighteen additional incredible figures from history. Some of them you may know, like the first black president of the United States or the man who said, "I have a dream," and some of them may be new to you, like the man who taught Charles Darwin about taxidermy or the first African American in space. Some of them even played an important role in the lives of the legends you've already read about. You'll find a nice balance if you are looking to learn about someone new or if you are eager to connect some dots!

If you want to discover more about these figures, check out the Further Reading section. It includes some great resources to get you going.

JOHN EDMONSTONE
Late 1700s–Unknown

Formerly enslaved in present-day Guyana, he taught Charles Darwin taxidermy at the University of Edinburgh. A world traveler, he told Charles about the wildlife in Guyana and elsewhere in South America, and this may have influenced Charles to study natural history.

VICENTE GUERRERO
1782–1831

Born a peasant in Mexico, he was a leader in the insurgent army against Spanish rule and helped win his country's independence in 1821. He became Mexico's second president in 1829 and levied taxes to help the poor and abolished slavery.

W. E. B. DU BOIS
1868–1963

An intellectual and activist, he helped form the NAACP in 1909 in order to fight for civil rights for black people. He helped found the *Crisis* magazine and wrote many books about racism and its effects, including the classic *The Souls of Black Folk*, which is still widely read today.

GEORGE DIXON
1870–1909

Considered by many to be the greatest fighter of the nineteenth century, he was the first black world champion in any sport and the first Canadian boxing champion. A fast and clever fighter, he held the bantamweight and featherweight crowns.

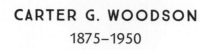

CARTER G. WOODSON
1875–1950

A voracious learner, he traveled the
world and met many different people.
He realized how important remembering
the past was to understanding the
present. He started Negro History Week
in 1926, which became Black History
Month, and wrote many books
about black history.

FREDERICK "FRITZ" POLLARD
1894–1986

The first African and Native American
head coach in what would become the
NFL. He was the first black player to take
part in the Rose Bowl, in 1916 with Brown
University, and to win a championship,
in 1920 with the Akron Pros.
Nicknamed "the Human Torpedo."

ROBERT "WHIRLWIND" JOHNSON
1899–1971

The first black doctor given practice rights at Lynchburg General Hospital. He also created a free junior tennis program for black kids, to teach positive values and desegregate tennis in Virginia. His most famous students were Althea Gibson and Arthur Ashe.

BAYARD RUSTIN
1912–1987

An early leader of the Civil Rights Movement and an openly gay man, he mentored Martin Luther King Jr. and introduced him to non-violent protest. He was one of the main organizers of the March on Washington for Jobs and Freedom in 1963.

NELSON MANDELA
1918–2013

As a member of the African National Congress, he fought against apartheid in South Africa. This led to twenty-six years of imprisonment. Under pressure by anti-apartheid groups worldwide, the government freed him in 1990. Nelson helped end apartheid and was elected president of South Africa in 1994.

JACKIE ROBINSON
1919–1972

Broke the color barrier in Major League Baseball (MLB) in 1947, winning the Most Valuable Player Award just two years later. His success in playing America's pastime showed that black people could excel if given an even playing field. He inspired people to fight for equality.

MEDGAR EVERS
1925–1963

As the NAACP field secretary in Mississippi, he organized boycotts of segregated white businesses and helped register black people to vote. He investigated the lynching of Emmett Till. Medgar's murder by a white supremacist energized many Mississippians and the nation to fight for civil rights.

MALCOLM X
1925–1965

When his family was targeted by white supremacists, young Malcolm turned to crime. In prison, he converted to Islam and became a spokesperson for the Nation of Islam. A lifelong student, he developed a philosophy of black empowerment and self-determination and advocated for human and civil rights.

BERRY GORDY
1929–

The founder of Motown, he helped popularize rhythm and blues and develop the sound for some of the most prominent artists of the 1960s and 1970s. He started the careers of the Temptations, Diana Ross and the Supremes, Stevie Wonder, and the Jackson 5.

MARTIN LUTHER KING JR.
1929–1968

One of the world's most prominent civil rights leaders and an inspiration to millions. As the president of the Southern Christian Leadership Conference, he pressured the US government into passing the Civil Rights Act of 1964 and the Voting Rights Act of 1965.

FLOYD NORMAN
1935–

As the first black animator at Disney, he worked on *Sleeping Beauty*, *Mulan*, *Toy Story 2*, and more. He co-founded Vignette Films to make movies about black history and has authored many books on cartooning, animation techniques, and the film industry.

GUION "GUY" BLUFORD
1942–

First African American in space, in 1983. He flew four space shuttle missions in nine years, logging 688 hours off the planet. He conducted many scientific experiments while in space, including studying the effects of spaceflight on the human body.

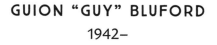

DJ KOOL HERC
1955–

One of the founders of hip-hop music. He developed the sound while DJing parties he threw in the Bronx, New York, in the 1970s. He invented the "merry-go-round" technique, using two turntables to extend a song's instrumental break.

BARACK OBAMA
1961–

The first black president of the United States, he was awarded the Nobel Peace Prize in his first term. He helped lead the country out of the 2008 Great Recession and signed the Affordable Care Act into law, making health care available to millions more citizens.

Further Reading,

WATCHING, AND LISTENING

My favorite place to start research on incredible people is straight from the source. I love watching them in interviews and reading autobiographies. This section is filled with resources, including books, music, and movies created by the talented men you just read about. You can use these tools to keep investigating and discovering long after you've finished this book.

READ THEIR WRITING

James Baldwin: *Little Man, Little Man: A Story of Childhood*

Frederick Douglass: *Narrative of the Life of Frederick Douglass*

Langston Hughes: *The Weary Blues*

Dwayne McDuffie: *Static Shock*

Leland Melvin: *Chasing Space (Young Readers' Edition)*

Barack Obama: *Of Thee I Sing: A Letter to My Daughters*

WATCH THEIR WORK

The Learning Tree (1969): Written and directed by Gordon Parks

Borom Sarret (1968): Written and directed by Ousmane Sembène

Static Shock (TV series, 2000–2004): Created by Dwayne McDuffie

The Symbol of the Unconquered (1920): Written and directed by Oscar Micheaux

HEAR THEIR MUSIC

Louis Armstrong: "What a Wonderful World" (1967)

Harry Belafonte: "The Banana Boat Song (Day-O)" (1955)

Chuck D: "Public Enemy No. 1" (1987)

Langston Hughes: *Weary Blues*, album by Charles Mingus, Langston Hughes, and Leonard Feather (1958)

Prince: "Purple Rain" (1984)

Paul Robeson: "Ol' Man River" (1936)

WATCH FILMS ABOUT THEM

I Am Not Your Negro (2016) (PG-13)

The Gospel According to André (2017) (PG-13)

Jazz: A Film by Ken Burns (2001)

Langston Hughes: Poet, Social Activist, Novelist, Playwright & Literary Giant (2016)

Mr. Civil Rights: Thurgood Marshall & the NAACP (2014)

READ BOOKS ABOUT THEM

Jabari Asim, with art by E. B. Lewis: *Preaching to the Chickens: The Story of Young John Lewis*

Jacob Lawrence, art, with poem by Walter Dean Myers: *The Great Migration: An American Story*

Vaunda Micheaux Nelson, with art by R. Gregory Christie: *Bad News for Outlaws: The Remarkable Life of Bass Reeves, Deputy U.S. Marshal*

Andrea Davis Pinkney, with art by Brian Pinkney: *Martin & Mahalia: His Words, Her Song*

Carole Boston Weatherford, with art by Eric Velasquez: *Schomburg: The Man Who Built a Library*

Carole Boston Weatherford, with art by Jamey Christoph: *Gordon Parks: How the Photographer Captured Black and White America*

WEBSITES FOR RESEARCH

Gordonparksfoundation.org

Mabonativetitle.com

Motownmuseum.org

NAACP.org

NASA.gov

Nmaahc.si.edu

Nobelprize.org

Nytimes.com/spotlight/ overlooked

SOURCES

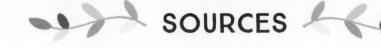

Ashe, Arthur, and Arnold Rampersad. *Days of Grace: A Memoir.* New York: Alfred A. Knopf, 1993.

Billingsley, Andrew. *Yearning to Breathe Free: Robert Smalls of South Carolina and His Families.* Columbia: University of South Carolina Press, 2007.

Brooks, Michael. *At the Edge of Uncertainty: 11 Discoveries Taking Science by Surprise.* New York: Abrams, 2016.

Burton, Art T. *Black Gun, Silver Star: The Life and Legend of Frontier Marshal Bass Reeves; A Reader.* Lincoln: University of Nebraska Press, 2006.

Cerami, Charles A. *Benjamin Banneker: Surveyor, Astronomer, Publisher, Patriot.* New York: John Wiley and Sons, 2002.

Fricke, Jim, and Charlie Ahearn. *Yes, Yes, Y'all: The Experience Music Project Oral History of Hip-Hop's First Decade.* Boston: Da Capo, 2002.

Gibson, Larry S. *Young Thurgood: The Making of a Supreme Court Justice.* Amherst, NY: Prometheus Books, 2012.

Goudsouzian, Aram. *King of the Court: Bill Russell and the Basketball Revolution.* Berkeley: University of California Press, 2010.

Gubert, Betty Kaplan, Miriam Sawyer, and Caroline M. Fannin. *Distinguished African Americans in Aviation and Space Science.* Westport, CT: Oryx Press, 2002.

Locke, Alain, ed. *Harlem, Mecca of the New Negro.* 1925. Reprint, Baltimore: Black Classic Press, 1980.

Melvin, Leland. *Chasing Space: An Astronaut's Story of Grit, Grace, and Second Chances.* New York: Amistad, 2017.

Ritchie, Andrew. *Major Taylor: The Extraordinary Career of a Champion Bicycle Racer.* Baltimore: Johns Hopkins University Press, 1996.

Tucker, Phillip Thomas. *Father of the Tuskegee Airmen, John C. Robinson.* Washington, DC: Potomac Books, 2012.

Wintz, Cary D. *Harlem Speaks: A Living History of the Harlem Renaissance.* Naperville, IL: Sourcebooks, 2007.

ACKNOWLEDGMENTS

In my introduction, I say this book almost didn't exist, and that is true on many levels. It took a lot of effort to bring all the moving parts together, and I asked so much of the people around me. I'm forever grateful to the LBYR team. It has been a dream to be able to make books with so many supportive and dedicated people. They've welcomed me into their offices and offered me grace and patience. Thank you to Jen Graham, Janelle DeLuise, Anna Prendella, Erika Schwartz, and Katharine McAnarney for all the hours and emails! Thank you also to Sandra Smith and Richard Slovak, as well as Anna Barnes at PRH in the UK.

Farrin Jacobs deserves all the awards. My friend and editor, she always goes above and beyond. Thank you for keeping me on track and indulging the cat talk. Creative director David Caplan and designer Kelly Brennan were tasked with so much, so quickly, but they were equal parts cool and professional, making this experience that much easier. My agent, Carrie Hannigan, is always here to steer this ship, even when the work gets overwhelming and the hours get crazy. I couldn't do it without her. Ellen Goff comes through even when I throw crazy curveballs at her. I'm wowed by her calm and efficiency.

Thank you to my family and friends: Chandra and Ted Harrison, Nicole Harrison, Lindsey Arturo, Ashley Chipman, Elena Levenson, Justen Blaize, and Roxanne Campbell.

Finally, thank you to my friend Kwesi Johnson. He's been behind the scenes as my on-call expert and sounding board on nearly all my books. I'm grateful for his willingness to help me tell the stories of these exceptional men. It was not easy, but fortunately with him it was still incredibly fun.   —VH

Thanks to my in-laws, Linda and Israel Garcia, for watching the kids, cleaning the house, and making meals while I was researching and writing. It takes a village to raise a child and a city to write a book, and those two are an army.

This book was a great opportunity to reexamine the black men I admired as a kid, shed light on those men I discovered as an adult, and discover new brothas to admire. Thanks to Vash and Farrin for giving me a shot and being patient with this old round head.

Thanks to my loving nuclear family—Jen, Luna, and Xolani—for supporting me. To my mom, Alyce, cousin Judy, uncle Ron, auntie Judy, and Charles: Thanks for helping me fill the holes in my research and raising me to love my blackness and black history.   —KJ

DRAW YOUR OWN LITTLE LEGEND

Since there were so many names that couldn't fit in the book, I'm giving you the opportunity to create your own Little Legend!

Use the following page to draw someone who you think is legendary. Who do you think is exceptional? It could be you or someone who inspires you—a friend, an adult you admire, or even a fictional character. Or it could be someone from history.

There's **Jesse Owens**, the four-time gold-medalist track star who proved Hitler wrong at the 1936 Summer Olympics. Or **Jean-Michel Basquiat**, the visionary young painter who in the 1980s elevated graffiti into the elite art world. What about **Mansa Musa**, one of the richest men in history? Or **Toussaint L'Ouverture**, the revolutionary who fought for Haiti's freedom and made it the first independent country in the Caribbean?

Consider some jazz legends like pianist **Duke Ellington**, trumpeter **Miles Davis**, or saxophonist **Charlie "Bird" Parker**. Or playwright **August Wilson**, activist **Marcus Garvey**, explorer **Matthew Henson**...the list goes on and on!

When I draw, I start out with a few simple steps. First I ask, If I were going to dress up in a costume to look just like this person, what would I wear? How would I style my hair? Are there any distinguishing features like freckles or a big, bushy mustache? Next, I think about key moments in the person's life, to draw something in the background to identify a particular time or place. For Matthew Henson, maybe something snowy and icy to look like the North Pole. And last, I like to find out if there are important items or accessories the person might hold or that I might put in the surrounding doodles: a paintbrush for Jean-Michel Basquiat and gold medals for Jesse Owens.

The best part is, there are no rules, so just have fun! Keep asking questions and keep learning!

Nicole Harrison

VASHTI HARRISON is an artist and filmmaker with a passion for storytelling. She earned her BA in studio art and media studies from the University of Virginia and her MFA in film/video from California Institute of the Arts, where she snuck into animation and illustration classes to learn from Disney and DreamWorks legends. There she rekindled a love for drawing and painting. Now she uses her love of both film and illustration to craft beautiful stories for children.

@vashtiharrison ✶ vashtiharrison.com